Learning Ballet

This book was given to me by:

_____

_You can
put a photo
of yourself here._

My name: _____

My birthday: _____

My address: _____

_____

LEARNING

BALLET

Katrin Barth & Sigrid Roemer

Sports Science Consultant: Dr. Berndt Barth

Meyer & Meyer Sport

Original Title: *Ich lerne Ballett & Tanz*
© Aachen: Meyer & Meyer, 2006
Translated by Petra Haynes
AAA Translation, St. Louis, Missouri, USA
www.AAATranslation.com

British Library Cataloguing in Publication Data
A catalogue record for this book is available from the British Library

Learning Ballet
Katrin Barth /Sigrid Roemer
Oxford: Meyer & Meyer Sport (UK) Ltd., 2007
ISBN 978-1-84126-224-6

© 2008 by Meyer & Meyer Sport (UK) Ltd.
Aachen, Adelaide, Auckland, Budapest, Graz, Indianapolis, Johannesburg,
New York, Olten (CH), Oxford, Singapore, Toronto
Member of the World

Sports Publishers' Association (WSPA)
www.w-s-p-a.org
Printed and bound by: B.O.S.S Druck und Medien GmbH, Germany
ISBN 978-1-84126-224-6
E-Mail: verlag@m-m-sports.com
www.m-m-sports.com

TABLE OF CONTENTS

Please note:
The exercises and practical suggestions in this book have been carefully chosen and reviewed by the authors. However, the authors are not liable for accidents or damages of any kind incurred in connection with the content of this book.

I LOVE TO GLIDE THROUGH THE AIR ···

..... OR TWIRL IN A CIRCLE TO BEAUTIFUL MUSIC.....

SOME SYMBOLS YOU WILL SEE A LOT IN THIS BOOK

When you see me with a thumbs-up, I have a good tip or suggestion for you.

When you see me with a question mark, there is a brainteaser or a tricky question. You can find the solutions at the back of the book in the solutions chapter.

When I hold a pencil in my hand, there is something to fill in or color. Have fun with it!

When you see me jumping, you will find exercises you can do at home. Don't forget to warm up first!

The exercise manikins

The little exercise manikins show you what you can try out at home. Pay close attention to the exercise description and don't forget to warm up first.

Once you have tried the exercise, you can color in the corresponding flower. You can start with this blossom.

The mistake manikins

The purple manikins are always doing something wrong when performing a movement. Look at them carefully. Can you find the mistake? Sometimes we really exaggerate in the drawing!

You can find the solution on the solutions page at the back of the book.

Would you like to color me? If this book is yours, then pick up your crayons and get started! Finish the drawing!

1 DEAR DANCER

What happens when you hear beautiful music, a melody plays and you feel the rhythm? Maybe you feel like you need to move to the beat; you want to twirl around, lift your arms and leap! Sometimes these movements are light, as though you were floating. Sometimes you want to spin wildly, stomp or jump.

Dance lets you express your emotions and tell stories. You can dress up and slip into another role. Maybe you become a frightened bunny, a beautiful princess, or a dangerous wizard. Together with other children, you diligently prepare for your big performance. Your parents, siblings and grandparents will be amazed at what you have already learned.

Many girls and boys enroll at ballet schools, music schools or sports clubs, to learn the most important movements from dance instructors. Together with other children, they enjoy the music and the movements. But good dance instruction is also important for gymnasts, figure skaters and athletes from other sports, to practice their particular sport.

In this dance book, we have listed some interesting facts about your favorite activity. We explain the most important movements, how you can practice them, and which mistakes to avoid. You will receive many suggestions for practicing alone or with your friends.

13

Here are some of the reasons children like to dance.
Which ones apply to you? Check "YES" or "NO"!

	YES	NO
I love to move.	☐	☐
I like being with other children.	☐	☐
I enjoy listening to music.	☐	☐
I want to transform myself and slip into other roles.	☐	☐
I am flexible and therefore probably well suited.	☐	☐
I can twirl fast and jump high.	☐	☐
I have a good sense of rhythm.	☐	☐
I like to watch ballet.	☐	☐
My friends also dance.	☐	☐
I want to be better than others.	☐	☐
I want to dance big parts on stage.	☐	☐
I want to be really famous.	☐	☐

If you answered the majority of questions with a "YES" then dancing is
right for you!

There are also many ideas for dancing. Of course Mom, Dad, your grandparents, siblings, and anyone else who, like you, enjoys it is invited to practice. Maybe you will be a professional dancer some day and will be one of the super-successful dancers who can be seen on stage or on television. But even if dance remains a recreational activity for you, you will enjoy it.

You will practice together with others, become part of a group, or sometimes even take center stage. You learn to practice diligently and to have willpower when things get tough. You won't always be the best. Sometimes it happens that you mess up on a turn, miss a cue or move in the wrong direction. But soon you will notice that regular practice is giving you more endurance, making you more flexible, rhythmic and stronger. Your body is fit and healthy.

This little book is meant to be your companion as you learn to dance. If we ever state something differently from the way your instructor explains it, that can happen sometimes. Just ask questions! In ballet and dance, opinions often differ.

Have fun dancing!
The authors and Gracie the butterfly.

15

Here you can paste a pretty dance photo of yourself.

2 PEOPLE HAVE ALWAYS WANTED TO DANCE

When did people begin to dance? No one knows for sure. But surely dancing has been around for as long as there have been people.

Dancing provides people with a wonderful tool to express their emotions and thoughts. They can communicate to others what they are feeling and their state of being. Dancing together connects people.

All around the world there is dance. Over many centuries, every country and culture has developed typical dances of its own. They are part of people's traditions.

Aside from these dances, many exhibition dances also developed. These are performed on a stage for the entertainment of an audience.

WHY PEOPLE DANCE

Not only in the early days, but even now there are specific dances for special occasions. Here we have compiled some reasons for such dances. Of course there are many more opportunities for dancing.

(Ancient) religious dances

People dance these dances to worship their gods. They want to please the gods and in difficult situations ask for their help. In their dances they ask for rain, a good harvest, a successful hunt, many children, or good health for their family.

The dancers paint their faces and bodies and wear elaborate costumes.

War dances

Warriors danced before they went into battle. With fierce masks and holding their weapons, they wanted to reassure each other and ask for help from the gods.

At the same time, small battles would sometimes be re-enacted.

Celebratory dances

A child is born, a couple gets married, or the new village schoolhouse is finished. People have always found reasons for a celebratory dance.

Dances were also performed for the new chief or an important visitor to the community.

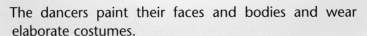

Dancing as entertainment

People also dance for fun and to entertain an audience. Good dancers in beautiful costumes dance on a stage and delight the audience.

There are also theater dances that tell stories.

Artisan dances

The clothiers dance the flag dance, the cobblers dance the cobblers' dance and the shepherds the shepherds' dance.

Time and again, guilds (or professions) find a good reason to perform their particular dances.

Courtship dances

Men want to be liked by women and women want to be liked by men. There are dances that let them display their beauty, grace and strength. Men and women court each other, flirt and want to find a marriage partner.

Seasonal dances

Important events determine the course of the year. These include recurring celebrations and their dances. There are dances for the Mardi Gras parade, the spring festival, a carnival, summer solstice or Halloween.

19

NATIONAL DANCES

In every country, particular dances have developed to music that is characteristic of a region. The music is played with special instruments and the dancers wear the traditional garb of their country.

Maybe you are familiar with such dances from your vacations. When such national dances are performed, they are also referred to as ethnic dances. But they often just serve as entertainment and have little to do with their actual origins.

GERMANY
WALTZ

AUSTRIA
POLKA

HUNGARY
CSÀRDÀS

POLAND
MAZURKA
KRAKOWIAK

HOLLAND
CLOG DANCE

ITALY
TARANTELLA

RUSSIA
KASATSCHOK

FRANCE
CAN-CAN

GREECE
SIRTAKI

SPAIN
FLAMENCO

TURKEY
BELLY DANCE

USA
SQUARE DANCE

Of course every country has even more beautiful dances. Dancers often like to try the different dances from other countries.

ALWAYS NEW DANCES

People have passed on their old dances from generation to generation and always enjoyed dancing them. In addition there were also modifications, changes, new steps and other dance moves. Thus many more dances evolved.

The type of music, the costumes and the settings have also continued to evolve. Of course this also has something to do with the fashion of the time. Today, artists sometimes use the most advanced technology for their music, lighting, and stage design.

CLASSICAL BALLET

Ballet is a particular form of dance and was created in the courts of Italian princes about 500 years ago. A royal dance academy was later founded in France. Russia also has a long-standing tradition of classical ballet.

Some dancers have become famous and are real stars.

Ballet is an art form of the stage, like plays or opera. Until a hundred years ago, classical ballet was also the only form of dance performed on the stage.

Most of the classical ballet terms come from the French language.

21

Take a look at these images. Now write the first letter of each in the appropriate box.

The solution is the name for someone who comes up with the movements to music and the story for a dance performance.

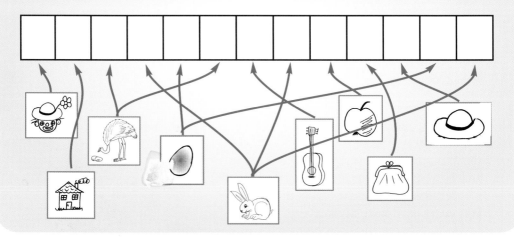

Oh boy! What happened here? Gracie made a list of her four favorite ballets, but the paper has been torn.

Can you piece it back together? Write the names on the blank lines!

BIRD

SWAN _____

NUT

BEAUTY

_____

FIRE

LAKE

_____

SLEEPING

CRACKER

_____

MODERN DANCE FORMS

Next to classical ballet, other dance forms also emerged. These include modern dance. Modern dance was created in the United States. But people in other parts of the world soon enjoyed these dance forms, too.

Other movements are:

Breakdance

Young people in big American cities bring their giant "boom boxes" out on the street and play loud music. To this they perform the wildest dances. These are acrobatic feats with contortions, spins and jumps. They even spin on their heads.

Electronic Boogie

The dancers move like robots. The dance moves are not smooth and round, but angular and choppy.

Jazz

In this type of modern dance the dancers move only one body part at a time, like the head, shoulders, pelvis, arms, or legs. This dance style is also a popular form of exercise.

23

Every symbol appears just once in each column, each row, and each diagonal. Draw the remaining symbols in the appropriate boxes!

Tina is watching Julie at practice. Then she asks her:
"I guess you like to dance?" "Sure!" says Julie.
"Then why don't you learn how?"

The dance instructor asks Tom:
"Why do you come to practice with dirty feet?"
"I don't have any others!" replies Tom.

3 HI THERE, BEATE!

Beate Gehrisch
Born on January 8, 1965, in Berlin, Germany
Dancer at the Leipzig Opera
Dance instructor at the Johann Sebastian Bach Music School Leipzig

Hi there, Beate! What do you like so much about dancing?

I love the music and can feel it with my entire body. Dance allows me to make this affinity visible. I can express many different emotions: joy and sorrow, love and hate, good and bad. Without words, only through movement can I tell an entire story that touches people.

What were your goals?

Like every little ballet girl, I wanted to become a dancer on a big stage. That is why I worked hard at every practice and gave it my all.

Regardless of whether you become a professional dancer or dance remains a hobby, it is only fun if you keep improving and continue to dance more!

What was your greatest and most important success?

I was allowed to study at a state ballet school and received my training as a professional dancer there. After graduation, I was able to dance at the Leipzig Opera in all the ballets I had always dreamt of as a child. There was "Swan Lake," "Sleeping Beauty," and "The Nutcracker," but also modern ballets like "Abraxas" and "Sacre du Printemps."

My involvement in the ballet creations of Uwe Scholz, who became the choreographer and ballet director at the Leipzig Opera in 1991, was a particular honor.

Did you sometimes not feel like practicing?

Actually I always liked to practice. But of course there were things I did not like to do as much, or that even frightened me. But when you have a goal, you can never give up under any circumstances! You have to be able to grit your teeth and bear it!

Did you have other hobbies as a child?

My sister and I had four parakeets, a turtle, fish and two mice. And we also had tons of books that I loved to read. Together we listened to lots of music and made up dances with our friends. Sometimes we gave small performances in homemade costumes.

What are you doing now?

I teach ballet at a big music school. I prepare the younger students for ballet classes and I train the older students in classical dance. I want to spark the fire of love for dance in every little dancer's heart. That isn't always easy, but it is lots of fun.

What advice do you have for young dancers?

You should always enjoy the movement. But that alone is not enough. Set goals and work to achieve them. Once you have chosen something, do it wholeheartedly. It is important to find the right school. Look at the classes and performances.

Arrange your day so you have some free time for other hobbies and friends after homework and dance practice.

Thank you very much for this conversation. We wish you continued luck and success with your dance students!

Have a dream and live it!

Beate Gehnrich

4 NO PAIN, NO GAIN

Have you ever dreamt of standing on a big stage? Everyone cheers, admires and marvels at you. All over town there are posters with your picture and every newspaper wants an interview with you. The biggest opera theaters, musicals, or ballet companies want to hire you.

Your dance style and grace are a dream; your spins are perfect and your jumps powerful. Every member of the audience is fascinated!

But wait! Just lying in the grass and dreaming of success is not enough!

If you want to become a good dancer, maybe even better than the others, you must practice often and diligently. That isn't always easy and isn't always fun right away either.

Success requires effort!

29

GOALS ARE IMPORTANT

When you begin with dancing, you need to think about the following things:

What is my goal? What do I want to achieve?

It really is fun to move to the music and feel the melodies. But soon you will want to be able to execute the movements more accurately, to form the step sequences more perfectly, and to stay on the beat.

You want to dance a good part in the Christmas performance – maybe even the principal part this time? Or maybe you want to finally be able to try on that princess costume or put on that scary mask?

Maybe you dream of dancing the beautiful classical parts in ballets like "The Nutcracker," "Sleeping Beauty," or "Swan Lake." Or you will become a perfect dancer in musicals or on television shows. Of course you are still too young for that. But nevertheless, you should already have some bigger goals now. You have to know what you want. If you don't have a goal, practicing soon won't be fun anymore. Big goals will propel you!

There are "small" and close goals:
    To be commended at the next dance lesson or to not get off beat.

There are also goals that are a little more distant:
    To dance a bigger part at the next performance or to get lots of applause.

And of course many dancers have the biggest goal of all:
    To attend a ballet school and become a professional dancer.

Why do you want to learn to dance?
Write down your goals here!

_____

_____

_____

_____

It is perfectly normal to have new and different goals over the course of your dancing years.

How can I reach my goal?

Now you might ask what you can do to improve your performance. You should definitely always go to dance practice and arrive on time. There you learn exercises for dance technique, endurance, physical fitness, strength, and flexibility. You dance with other children and learn to develop your sense of rhythm by dancing to music.

It is good to repeat certain exercises every day. The dance instructor will tell you which exercises are particularly important. Most likely there will be some things you won't enjoy doing that much. Some things may seem boring or much too strenuous. But you always have to remember that these exercises will help you achieve your goal.

Someone who wants to become a good dancer must be very diligent and goal-oriented!

What do I have to do to reach my goal?

How are things going now that you keep improving with lots of practice? As long as the exercises are easy and relaxed, the tendons and muscles will do only what they can already do anyway. Only when it is a little more strenuous and the stretches and movements aren't as easy to do will you feel the progress. But you have to work hard and exert yourself.

When you haven't been at dance practice for a while you will notice that you have gotten a little worse. You are not as flexible, the dance steps seem more difficult, and you get out of breath more quickly. Now it's time to catch up!

PHYSICAL FITNESS IS IMPORTANT

Oh, no! What's wrong with Gracie? After half an hour of dancing she is so exhausted that she can barely stand up! Has that ever happened to you? Do you get out of breath that easily and feel weak so quickly? Then you have to work on your physical fitness level!

What is physical fitness?

When you dance you are always moving, getting in positions, twirling and jumping. To do this you have to concentrate the entire time. Can you do that for a long time? Then you are physically fit.

If not, then dancing soon won't be much fun anymore. You have to do something to improve your fitness level. You can do that primarily by practicing regularly.

Gracie really wants to watch the performance, but now she has gotten lost in the theater's many corridors!

Can you show her the way to the stage?

STAGE

"Well, Anne, how was practice today?" asks Mother. "Great!" says Anne. "I must have been incredibly good, because the dance instructor had tears in her eyes!"

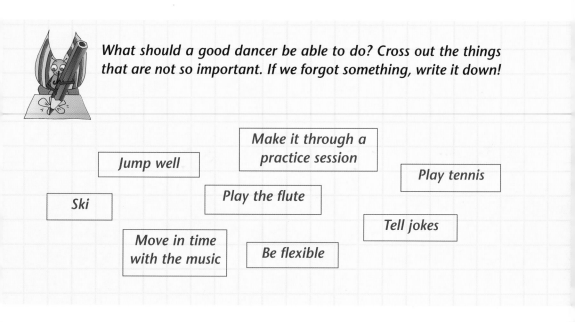

What should a good dancer be able to do? Cross out the things that are not so important. If we forgot something, write it down!

Make it through a practice session

Jump well

Play tennis

Ski

Play the flute

Tell jokes

Move in time with the music

Be flexible

What you must have

You must have endurance to be able to handle the physical strain for an extended period of time. You won't get winded as easily when you run, jump, bike, swim and especially dance. When you do something really strenuous, you recover quickly and are fit again. While you are dancing, you should always have an upright and taut posture. In addition, you will often have to bend your knees and lift your arms during the dance movements. That requires strength. Strong leg muscles let you jump high and far or spin fast. As you dance, you bend down very low, point your toes, and lift your legs very high. You get into a wide straddle or even do splits. For this, you need to be very limber and flexible.

Even during practice sessions, you won't spend the entire time dancing to beautiful music. There are many necessary exercises for improving your endurance, strength and flexibility.

Participate fully because it will help you get fit!

35

THIS IS HOW YOU CAN PRACTICE

Get moving!

- *Jog*
- *Bike*
- *Skateboard*
- *Swim*
- *Play basketball*
- *Play soccer*
- *Ski*
- *Hike*

and much more

Balance exercises

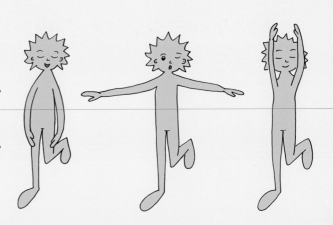

Stand on one leg

- Alternate legs – first the right, then the left.
- Close your eyes.
- Hold your arms out to the side, then overhead.

Stand on an unstable surface

Stand on an unstable surface and do exercises 1 and 2.

- Stand on a mat, a pillow, or a rolled-up blanket.
- Stand on a skinny (fallen) tree trunk.
- Stand on a "core board" or sports gyroscope.

With interference

Now incorporate some hindrances/difficulties into all of the exercises

- Balance an object in your hand.
- Balance an object on your head.
- Have someone toss you a ball, catch it and throw it back.
- Try throwing each other off balance by making each other laugh.
- Hold a band between you and pull. Who will get thrown off balance first?

Gracie is thrilled! She can hardly decide which of the beautiful flowers to land on. Only something is odd – the flowers don't have any color!

Did you do your exercises at home or play a sport? Then you can color these flowers. If there aren't enough flowers, draw some more!

5 WHAT YOU NEED FOR DANCING

Of course one can dance anywhere – in jeans and tennis shoes on the grass, in pajamas on the living room rug, or in a bikini and barefoot on the beach. You just need to enjoy moving to lively songs, pop music, or even to your own singing.

But when it comes to ballet and dance, the proper clothes are important. They should not only look nice, but you must be able to move well in them. The tightly fitted clothes allow your dance instructor to see your posture and the flexing of your muscles. The shoes make every move along with you and give you support.

But you don't need to buy special ballet outfits right away. In the beginning, a leotard, a bathing suit, a pair of tights or leggings, leg warmers and a sweatshirt are just fine. Some dance instructors even let you dance barefoot in the beginning.

You will find a good dance floor, a mirror and bars at your dance studio or music school.

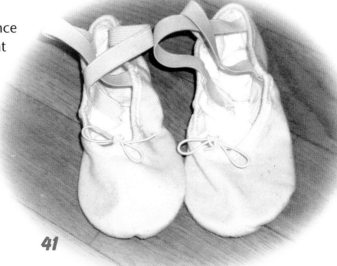

Suitable music is always chosen for the exercises. The beat and rhythm help you with the execution of the movements.

THE CLOTHES

A dancer should be able to move easily in her practice clothes. They should not interfere with her movements and should be neither too warm nor too cool. And of course she wants to be comfortable.

It is best to wear layers of clothes. This allows you to keep your muscles warm, and if you get too warm you can gradually undress, just like an onion with its many skins.

Dance clothes are always tightly fitted so the bodylines and muscles are visible.

Dance leotard

Wrap-around sweater

Tights

Leggings

Leg warmers

Your dance instructor determines what you wear to your practice sessions. Some dance groups wear uniform clothing.

THE DANCE SHOES

The dance shoes are made of fabric or leather. They have a special sole that supports the foot but is also flexible. Gymnastics slippers are not really suited for dancing because their soles are too wide.

Elastic bands hold the shoes firmly on the foot, so they don't slip off while you dance.

If the dance shoes you bought don't have elastic bands, you can sew some on yourself. The bands cross over, from the center seam to about the middle of the back of the shoe.

Modern dance is often danced *barefoot*. Jazz dancers wear *jazz shoes*. Tap dancing requires special *tap dancing shoes* whose toes and heels are reinforced with metal. That's how the shoes make that "tapping" sound on the floor.

Take good care of your dance shoes! They should be worn only for dancing and not on the street!

ADOLESCENTS AND ADULTS HAVE SUFFICIENTLY STRONG BONES AND MUSCLES. THEY ALSO DANCE ON THEIR TOES AND NEED SPECIAL BALLET SHOES WITH A REINFORCED TOE CAP. THESE SHOES FOR TOE DANCING ARE LACED WITH RIBBONS.

Which hairstyle will the dancer choose today?

Surely you have a favorite hairstyle that looks pretty and is practical. Add a photo of yourself to this page.

THE HAIR

Long hair, nice bangs, or wild curls are pretty, but are bothersome while dancing. You are constantly blowing strands of hair away from your face or pushing them behind your ear.

And it gets pretty hot while practicing!

While dancing you want to show the eyes and facial expression. That is why there should be no hair in the face. Pinned up hair shows off the nice shape of the neck and back.

You can pin up or braid long hair into many pretty hairstyles. Barrettes or headbands keep bangs away from the face.

Some ballet studios, dance schools, etc., have strict hairstyle guidelines.

45

THE DANCE STUDIO

The mirror

The mirror is important so dancers can always observe their posture and movement.

Please note: No looking in the mirror all the time and getting distracted!

The floor

The dance floor absorbs movements and provides footing so the dancers don't slide. The surface can be parquet or dance carpet.

Please note:
Never walk on the dance floor with street shoes.

The bar

The dancer can hold on to the bar (also called barre) so she doesn't lose her balance during the exercises.

Please note:
Don't hang on the bar!

THE MUSIC

The music is a very important component of nearly all dances. Ethnic dance groups dance to accordion music, African dancers dance to the sound of drums, or flamenco dancers dance to guitar rhythms. Flutes often accompanied medieval dances and pop music is played on modern dance shows. The composers of famous classical ballets wrote the music for large orchestras with many different instruments.

Maybe you can think of many other musical examples of this type. The music backs the dancers' movements. The choice of instruments depends on the type of dance.

The music in a dance class is almost always played from a CD. This allows the dance instructor to choose the ideal music for the exercises and dances. There are slow, fast, classical or modern pieces of music.

Some children are fortun-
ate enough to have a pianist accompany them with their exercises. He is called a **répétiteur**.

The répétiteur can adjust the speed and the rhythm as needed for dancing and exercises.

EVERYTHING PACKED?

You are very excited because today is your big performance. You have worked for many weeks to make sure everything works. The costumes and the set are beautiful.

Now imagine you arrive at the performance location, stand in the changing room, empty your bag, and … where are my shoes? Your beautiful new dance shoes that go so well with your costume are at home – far away! Left behind!

How will you dance your part now? You can't dance barefoot because that doesn't suit your part. The audience would wonder and you would spoil the nice performance for your dance group.

THE CHECKLIST

Do you know that anxious feeling that you are forgetting something? Or has it even happened to you already?

To ensure a great performance it is important to pack everything in plenty of time. Pack your bag the night before, so you can go to bed with your mind at rest.

A checklist could help you, too. Written on the list is everything you want to pack. Once it is actually in the bag, you can check it off. If you cannot read or write yet, draw a little picture of all the items.

Your parents can of course help you pack your bag, but every dancer is responsible for his things.

MY CHECKLIST

☐ LEOTARD

☐ TIGHTS

☐ DANCE SHOES

☐ HAIR TIES, BARRETTES, COMB

☐ WARM TOP

☐ LEG WARMERS, SOCKS

☐ TOILETRIES

☐ SOMETHING TO DRINK

☐ _____

☐ _____

☐ _____

☐ _____

Use the blank lines to write down anything else you mustn't forget.

All of the hair ties come in pairs. That means there are always two identical ones. Only one hair tie is unique. Can you find it?

Which part of the shoe is missing?
Find the right piece!

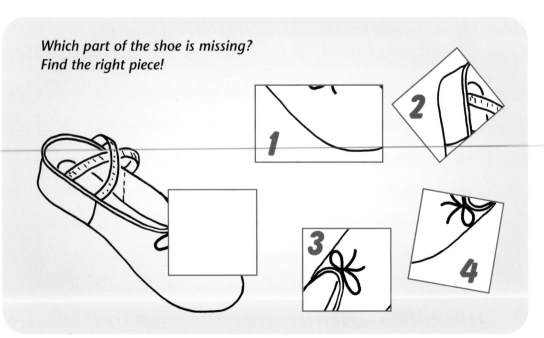

6 THE BODY AND ITS MOVEMENTS

You want to dance, twirl, stretch, bend, jump, and much more. Your movements should be lovely and graceful.

To do so you stand up tall or bend very low. You can extend or angle your knees, feet, and hands. The movements are light or powerful, fast or gentle.

That is why it is important that you know your body well. What does it feel like when the back is straight? How far forward can I bend? How high can I jump?

You will be amazed how much you will discover about yourself and your body. And you will be surprised to see which movements you'll already be able to do after diligent practice.

51

BODY LANGUAGE

With your posture and your movements, you can also express how you feel.

Happy

You jump, leap, and twirl. Anyone can see how happy you are.

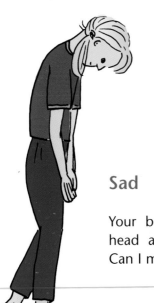

Sad

Your back is rounded and your head and shoulders are droopy. Can I make you feel better?

Proud

Your erect body and the position of your arms alone show how proud you are. Add to that the raised nose and the confident look. Or may be you are just offended or feel hurt?

Strength

Look at me—my muscles and the tough look on my face! Standing as tall as you can with your chest puffed out, you show that no one messes with you.

MAYBE YOU HAVE SEEN THAT DANCERS USE CERTAIN GESTURES TO EXPRESS THEIR FEELINGS.

IN LOVE:
HANDS AGAINST THE HEART

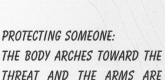

PLEADING, BEGGING:
PALMS TOGETHER AS IN PRAYER

PROTECTING SOMEONE:
THE BODY ARCHES TOWARD THE THREAT AND THE ARMS ARE EXTENDED BACK.

53

WHAT YOU CAN DO WITH YOUR BODY

You can move the parts of your body into different positions. Like stretching your fingers, hands, and arms really long, but also making them round. This also works with the back. Wrists, elbows, and knees can be bent at various angles and extended.

Really tall

Now make yourself really tall! You want to be the tallest of all. Feel your feet flat against the floor and then straighten up as far as you can. Be careful not to raise your shoulders when you extend your arms overhead.

Very small and round

Imagine you had to hide in a small box. Would you be able to fit in it? Coil up as tightly as you can and press your arms, legs, and head against your body.

Really wide

Who can take up the most space with his body? Make yourself wide and spread your fingers and toes.

55

MOVING TO MUSIC

You can express how you feel with your posture and your movements. Your movements can be as varied as the music.

Happy and fast music

You will want to jump, twirl, and clap your hands.

Slow and quiet music

This music is good to dream to. Your movements become very delicate, as though you were floating.

Wild and loud music

Boisterous and high-spirited, you can express any emotions. You want to jump, spin around and make silly movements.

Choose the music that matches your mood. And then dance to it – the way you feel!

7 THE PRINCIPLES OF DANCE

What is better than moving to music? You want to spin, bend, stretch, and jump. The movements of your arms and legs look smooth and light.

But your body must be prepared for all of the dance movements. That is why you learn the important movements and practice them again and again. We refer to these movements as *the principles of dance.*

On the following pages you will find important principles of dance that you will learn in dance class. Here you can review the drawings at your leisure and read the information.

The illustrated mistakes will help you recognize mistakes, and on the practice pages you will find exercises you can also do at home. Don't forget to warm up.

ERECT POSTURE

In everyday life, how can you tell if a boy or a girl takes dance lessons? You might say: "I can tell by the erect posture!"

A dancer stands very erect, with a straight back, and very tall. This is how she can dance best.

You have to practice a lot for the erect posture, too. Sometimes you will think: "I am straight; I can't get any straighter!" But a glance in a mirror or at a photo sometimes still shows droopy shoulders, a hollow back, or a bend in the hip!

But not to worry! With lots of practice, you will get the right feel for your body!

THE ERECT POSTURE IS PREREQUISITE TO ALL POSITIONS IN CLASSICAL BALLET.

THE DANCERS MUST ALWAYS PAY ATTENTION TO THE STRAIGHT BACK, THE EXTENDED NECK, AND THE FORWARD GLANCE.

In the erect body position, this is what you should pay attention to:

Next to the drawing are some important instructions. Pay particular attention to these things while practicing.

WHAT ARE THESE MANIKINS DOING WRONG?

Take a good look at these drawings. Figure out why the mistake manikins don't have good posture. What are they doing wrong?

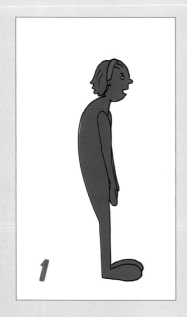

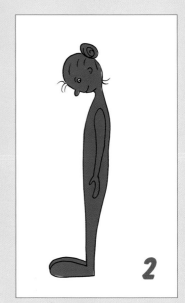

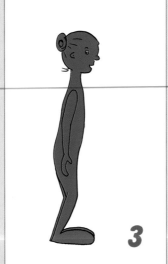

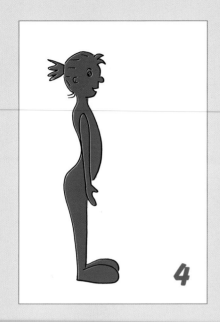

4

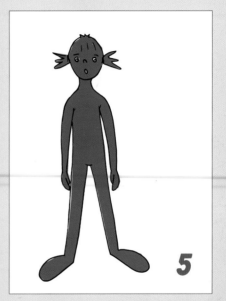

5

6

TRY IT OUT

Here are some exercises that you can also do at home. Maybe your siblings, friends or parents would like to participate.

Stretching out

Maybe you sometimes stretch in bed in the morning, after your mom wakes you up. You are still so tired and stretching helps you to wake up.

Of course you can also do this standing up.

Erect posture

Droopy shoulders show that you are sad. Or maybe your back is tired. Wake it up! Stretch out your back really long and tall and let your arms hang at your sides.

Imagine you are wearing a crown on your head. But beware – no hollow back!

Erect posture while sitting down

Sit down with your legs extended in front of you. Your back is very straight. Put a basket or something similar on top of your head.

 To avoid making a hollow back

Lie on your back, bend your knees, and plant your feet firmly on the floor. Your arms are extended alongside your body. Breathe evenly, and when you exhale you can feel your body spread out.

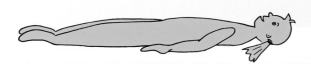

Now try to slowly extend your legs without your back leaving the floor.

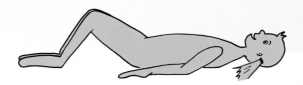

Now stand up straight. Imagine that the floor is still immediately behind you. Your body is now very erect. Can you feel it?

 **Once you have tried an exercise, you can fill in the flower with a pretty color.**

STRAIGHTENING THE LEGS

You have to learn to let your legs fully extend.

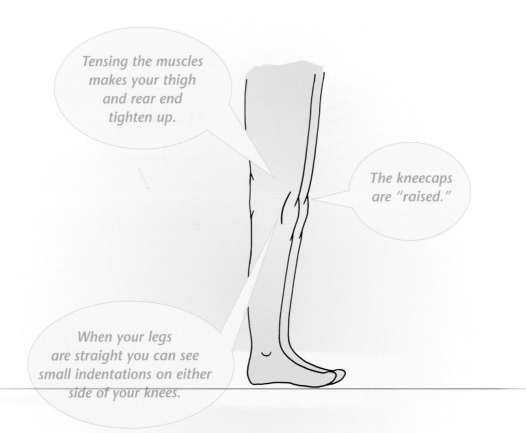

Tensing the muscles makes your thigh and rear end tighten up.

The kneecaps are "raised."

When your legs are straight you can see small indentations on either side of your knees.

Stand in front of a mirror with bare legs. Now look at what happens when you tense your muscles to straighten your legs. Can you see the little creases?

POINTED AND FLEXED FEET

A dancer needs his feet for many dance movements. That is why they have to be very flexible and pliant.

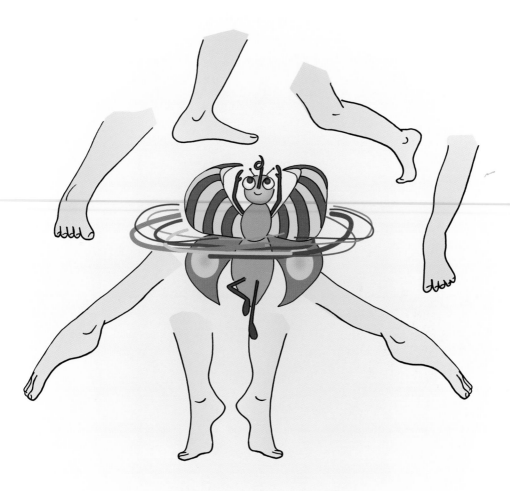

A dancer must be able to extend (point) and angle (flex) his feet very well.

TRY IT OUT

Point and flex your feet

How far you are able to point and flex your feet depends on how your body is built. But you can still get better with lots of practice.

1 *Sit on the floor with your legs extended in front of you. Your feet and ankles form a straight line. Don't turn your toes in or out! Imagine your legs are a long ribbon, all the way to your toes.*

2 *Now keep the feet extended long, but flex your toes.*

Spread your toes a little and your feet will look really wide.

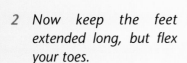

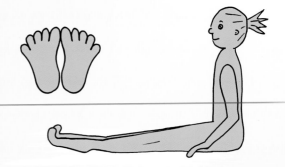

Try to also straighten the lower part of your back while you are sitting with your legs extended in front of you. That is often difficult because it always "wants" to be round!

3   Keep your legs extended in front of you, but flex your feet.

The toes are sticking in the air,
"looking at you."

4   Now bend your toes. They are now
    "looking" at the floor.

5   Now try to point your toes. Your
    feet should stay really long.

Now when you flex your feet again, you return to the starting position.

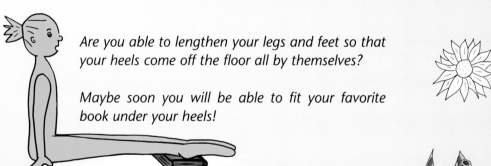

*Are you able to lengthen your legs and feet so that
your heels come off the floor all by themselves?*

*Maybe soon you will be able to fit your favorite
book under your heels!*

**Once you have tried an exercise, you can fill in the flower with
a pretty color.**

THE LEG POSITIONS

Almost all dance moves, including modern dance, begin and end with certain foot positions. It is easier to execute the movements in these positions and the body is always properly balanced.

In each leg position, you stand with your weight on both feet. You have to make sure that you don't stand on the outside or inside edges of your feet.

IF I SPREAD MY WINGS,
I WON'T FALL OVER!
THAT'S A GREAT IDEA!

Here we will show you what the positions should ideally look like. But everyone's leg and foot shapes are very different. Try it as best you can.

PARALLEL POSITION

In this position, the dancer stands very straight and holds his legs and feet together. The feet are very close together. You can feel your weight equally distributed over both feet.

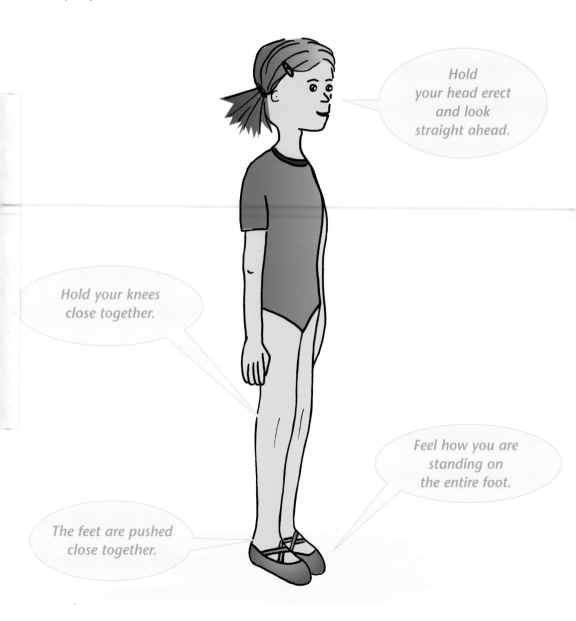

69

TURNOUT POSITION OF THE LEGS

Surely you have noticed that in many dance moves, the dancers' legs point to the outside. This leg position is called turnout.

The turning out motion starts in the hip joint.

To do this, the dancer must not only turn the feet, but she also turns out the thigh from the hip joint.

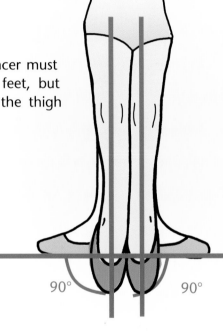

90°   90°

For someone who wants to become a ballet dancer, hip flexibility is very important. The dancers must be able to turn out their legs in the hip joint at a 90° angle. (Just like the drawing!) At ballet schools, this ability is tested with aptitude tests.

The turnout position of the legs depends primarily on your physical structure. Whether you will be able to do a big turnout of the legs through lots of practice, or in spite of all your efforts are still only able to do a smaller turnout, is important. Few people are able to do a 90° angle turnout.

Of course, you can still dance even if you are not that flexible. Not everyone has to become a ballet dancer!

FOR THE MORE ADVANCED BALLET DANCERS, THERE ARE ADDITIONAL IMPORTANT LEG POSITIONS. IF YOU CONTINUE TO PRACTICE FOR MANY YEARS, YOU WILL LEARN THESE, TOO.

3. Position

EN TROISIÈME

4. Position (open)

EN QUATRIÈME OUVERTE

4. Position (crossed)

EN QUATRIÈME CROISÉE

5. Position

EN CINQUIÈME

Why should the dancer turn the legs and feet out?

There is a very simple reason for the turnout of the legs:

You can lift your leg higher when the leg is turned out!

Experienced ballet dancers who have been practicing for many years, can lift their legs very high.

71

1ST POSITION
(EN PREMIÈRE, PRONOUNCE: ON PRAM-E-AIR)

To do the first leg position, you turn your legs out from the hip joint, so that your knees and feet face to the side. At the same time, firmly push your heels and straightened knees together.

Hold your back and pelvis very erect.

The knees are firmly pushed together.

The feet are turned out.

You should feel your little toes against the floor.

Feel how you are standing on the entire foot.

In all positions, keep your back very straight and straighten the knees (raising).

2ND POSITION
(EN SECONDE, PRONOUNCE: ON SEC-AND)

In the second position, the feet are again turned out. Your feet are planted a little farther apart. The distance between the heels is approximately as long as your feet.

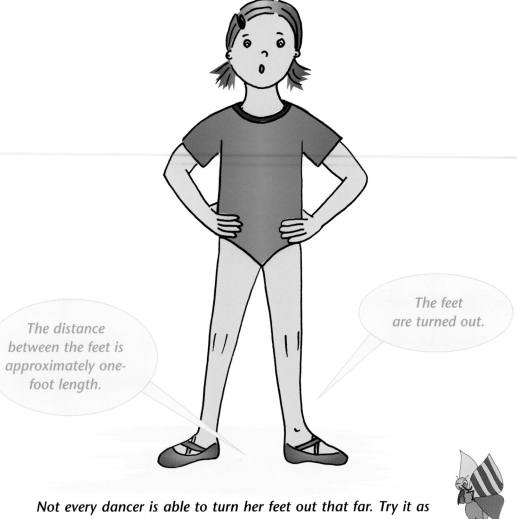

The distance between the feet is approximately one-foot length.

The feet are turned out.

Not every dancer is able to turn her feet out that far. Try it as best you can and keep practicing.

WHAT ARE THESE MANIKINS DOING WRONG?

Take a good look at these drawings. Figure out what the mistake manikins are doing wrong with the positions.

Mistakes in the parallel position

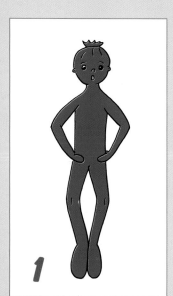

Don't be alarmed when the mistake manikins make such awful mistakes. In the drawings we always exaggerate a little so you can recognize the mistakes more easily.

Mistakes in the 1st position

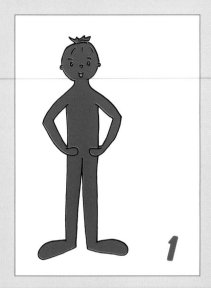

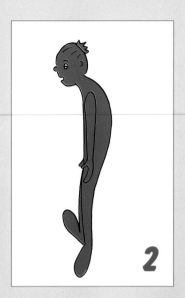

Mistakes in the 2nd position

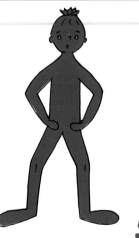

TRY IT OUT

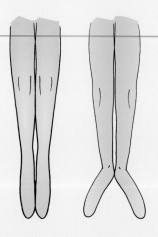

Sitting exercises

For these exercises, sit with your legs extended in front of you. Knees and feet are held tightly together. Imagine that not even a sheet of paper can fit between your knees. The hands barely touch the floor.

Start with the turnout from the hip joint. Now try to turn your little toes toward the floor.

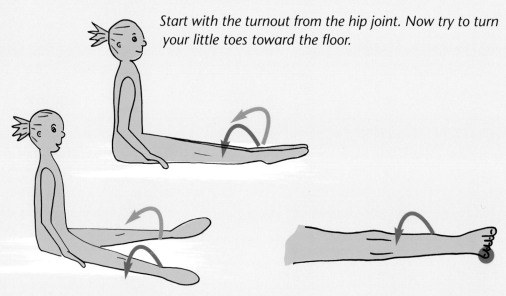

Lying down exercises

Once you are on your back, stretch yourself out. Keep your back flat against the floor, like you did with the exercises for the erect posture. Feel the floor beneath you and how the back spreads out!

Start again with the turnout from the hip joint. Try to turn your little toes toward the floor.

You can easily test for yourself why you need to turn the legs and feet out for the leg movement. You will feel that the hip blocks a higher lift when the feet are turned in. Try the following:

Lay on your side. The lower arm is extended overhead. The head rests on it. Now try to first lift the upper leg with the foot turned to the inside and then to the outside.

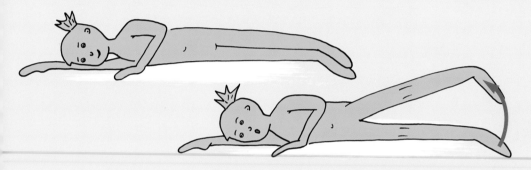

1   The upper leg is not turned out. You will notice that it doesn't go up very high.

2   Now turn the upper leg out from the hip joint. Now the knee and foot are turned out.

    What do you notice now when you lift your leg?

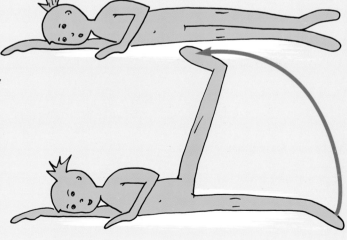

BENDING THE KNEES
(DEMI-PLIÉ, PRONOUNCE: DEMI PLEA-AY)

For this movement you bend your knees until you notice that your heels want to come up off the floor. (But that should not happen!)

After that you evenly straighten your knees until the kneecaps are raised up again.

For this movement, imagine you are an elevator that goes down and up very vertically. You have to keep your pelvis erect and don't let your torso tilt forward.

Think about how you wear a crown or a basket on your head.

VERY STRAIGHT UP AND DOWN – THAT'S HOW THE FENCE GETS A NEW COAT OF PAINT, AND I CAN DO MY EXERCISES!

In the parallel position

You start the exercises for the Demi-Plié from the parallel position. As you do this, you can rest your hands on your hips or leave your arms at your sides.

You stand tall and your back is straight.

Your pelvis is erect.

The knees stay closed.

The feet are closed. You are standing on the whole foot.

In the 2nd position

After the exercises in the parallel position, you first practice the Demi-Plié in the second position.

In the 1st position

After you have practiced in the parallel position and the second position, you now also do the Demi-Plié in the first position.

81

 *LEARNING BALLET*

WHAT ARE THESE MANIKINS DOING WRONG?

Take a good look at these drawings. What are they doing wrong with the Demi-Plié and the knee bends?

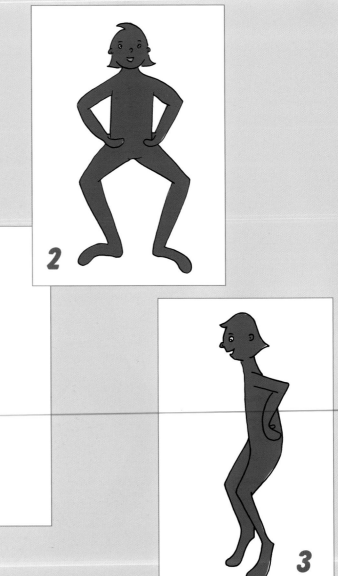

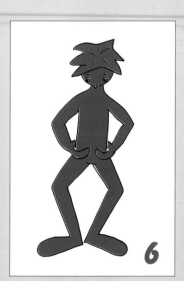

Pretty difficult! When you do the Demi-Plié you have to pay attention to so many things. And then not to fall over!

What are you having trouble with? Check the appropriate manikins for the things that you have to pay particular attention to!

83

TRY IT OUT

Try the knee bends in the parallel position first, then in the second position, and finally in the first position.

Exercise while holding on

Find something to hold on to so you don't lose your balance during the exercises. In the dance studio, you have the bar.

Maybe you can find a similar support at home.

For instance, the back of a chair works well.

Elevator

While you practice the Demi-Plié, imagine that you are in an elevator. You go down and up very straight.

With a "crown" on your head

Do you remember the exercise for erect posture? Put a basket, plastic bowl, or something similar on your head and then do the exercise.

Don't forget to color your flower!

RAISING UP ON THE BALLS OF THE FEET, HALF POINTE
(RELEVÉ, PRONOUNCE: RA-LA-VAY)

You stand very tall and erect. From this position, you lift your heels off the floor and stand on the balls of your feet. You will feel like a marionette that is being pulled straight up by a string.

From the parallel position

You stand tall and your back is straight.

The knees are raised. You can feel the indentations on the sides.

The legs are firmly held together.

The heels are firmly held together.

You stand on the balls of your feet.

As you inhale, make yourself as big as possible, extend your legs really long and lift your heels off the floor. Look straight ahead and hold yourself very straight. For this exercise you can also hold your arms out to the side. That will help you keep your balance.

If the knees aren't really straight and you are not standing erect, you will wobble or even fall over.

From the 2nd position   From the 1st position

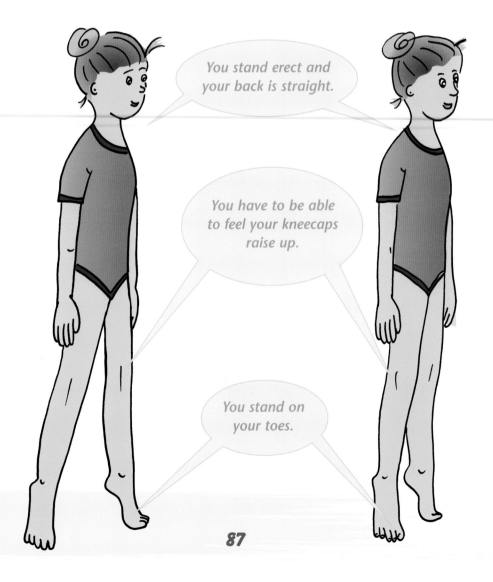

You stand erect and your back is straight.

You have to be able to feel your kneecaps raise up.

You stand on your toes.

BENDING OVER WHILE SITTING WITH THE LEGS EXTENDED FORWARD

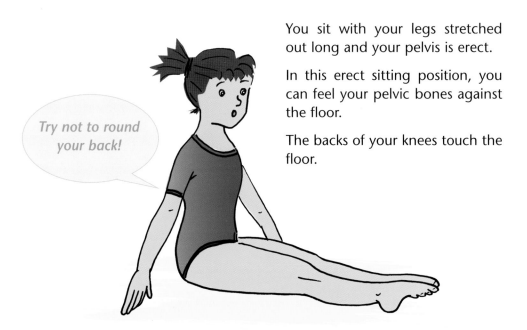

You sit with your legs stretched out long and your pelvis is erect.

In this erect sitting position, you can feel your pelvic bones against the floor.

The backs of your knees touch the floor.

Try not to round your back!

Now you bring your arms and hands to your knees. They creep forward, very slowly, all the way to your feet.

Make sure that your back stays very long and straight, and doesn't get round right away.

Your head and torso form a straight line, and your eyes are on your feet.

These imaginary lines form a triangle.

Can you touch your nose to your straightened knees?

It would be great if you could touch your torso to your thighs.

Try to exhale very deliberately in this position! With each breath, your torso should come forward just a little bit more!

BENDING OVER FROM A STANDING POSITION

To bend over from a standing position, get into the parallel position.

Now your head gets very heavy and you let your head droop down. Your torso also slowly bends down. Head and torso "flow" downward. The arms hang down low.

Bend over as far as you can. That can pull a little, but it should not hurt! At the same time, exhale and allow your body to hang this way for a moment. Feel how heavy your head and torso are.

Now straighten up again very slowly. As you do, "unroll" yourself. The head comes up last.

The torso comes down smoothly and supplely.

Can you touch the floor with your fingertips or maybe even with your palms?

Imagine your torso is a little brook that slowly ripples downward.

Bending over from 2nd position

You stand in second position and bend over. Carry this movement out the way we described for the parallel position.

Bending over from 1st position

You stand in first position and bend over. Carry the bending movement out the way we described for the parallel position.

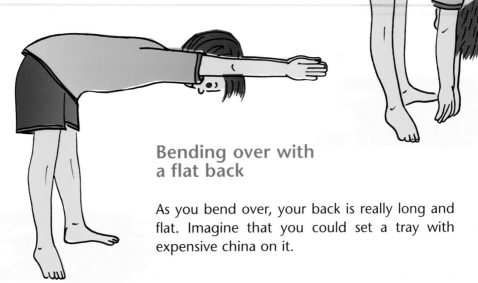

Bending over with a flat back

As you bend over, your back is really long and flat. Imagine that you could set a tray with expensive china on it.

Always make sure that the kneecaps are raised and the feet, even the little toes, are firmly on the floor.

It can pull a little in the legs, but it should not hurt!

WHAT ARE THESE MANIKINS DOING WRONG?

Figure out why the manikins are not bending over correctly in sitting position with legs extended forward and while standing. What are they doing wrong?

Mistakes with bending over in sitting position with legs extended forward.

1

2

Mistakes with bending over from a standing position

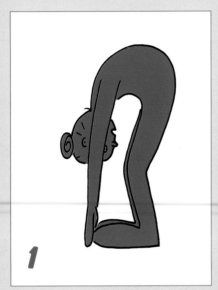

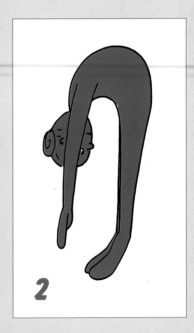

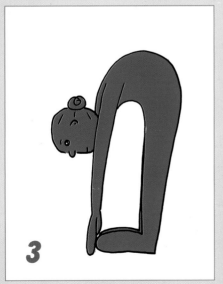

If you cannot figure out everything, look on the solutions page.

95

TRY IT OUT

Whenever you do stretching exercises, you have to warm up first. If your muscles and tendons are too cold and not prepared, you can pull them when you stretch. That hurts!

Imagine your body is a piece of modeling clay, that can't be formed into beautiful figures until it is soft and supple.

Bending over from a sitting position with legs extended forward

You sit with your legs extended in front of you and bend over. Your fingertips slowly work their way down to your feet. Can you already reach the tips of your toes? Does your nose touch your knees? Is your torso touching down on your thighs? Your hands want to reach your pointed feet and clasp them.

How far down on the floor can I go?

Stand up very straight. Now bend over easily and smoothly. You flow down to the floor like a little brook.

Do your fingertips reach the floor? Or even your palms? With lots of practice, you will continue to go lower.

Let yourself fall fast

Try letting your body drop down very fast. Clap your hands three times overhead and then three times on the floor.

But no cheating – keep your knees nice and straight!

From a squat

Get in a squat position and "glue" your fingertips or palms to the floor directly in front of your feet. Now slowly straighten your legs. Your rear end will be the highest point of your body.

Now "glue" the fingertips or the entire palm next to the feet. Extend your legs and straighten up.

Be careful not to fall over during any of these exercises!

SUPPORTING LEG AND FREE LEG

For many dance moves, you stand on just one leg. This leg is called the **supporting leg**. The supporting leg has to support the entire body weight.

The other leg is the **free leg**. You can lift this leg easily and loosely, bounce it up and down, drag it, and much more.

The leg you stand on is called **the supporting leg**.

The leg that moves is called **the free leg**.

In the beginning, you won't always be able to keep your balance. You will sometimes still wobble during the exercises.

But over the course of many practice sessions, you will learn to keep your center of gravity over your supporting leg.

When you want to stand on one leg, you must keep your pelvis and torso very erect. This will make your supporting leg really straight.

ARABESQUES ARE FAMOUS AND BEAUTIFUL FIGURES IN CLASSICAL BALLET.

THE WEIGHT IS SHIFTED TO THE SUPPORTING LEG AND THE FREE LEG IS LIFTED IN THE AIR. THIS CAN ALSO BE DONE TO THE FRONT OR TO THE SIDE.

TO BE ABLE TO MAKE THIS POSITION LOOK SO EASY, THE DANCERS MUST PRACTICE A LOT AND THEY MUST HAVE A GOOD SENSE OF BALANCE.

DRAGGING THE FOOT
(BATTEMENT TENDU, PRONOUNCED: BUT-MON-TON-DU)

In this movement, you drag your foot across the floor until only the big toe still touches the floor, and your free foot is pointed. At the same time, your posture is erect and both knees are straight. After that, drag the foot back to its starting position.

You practice the Battement Tendu first in the parallel position and then in first position.

Both legs remain straight.

You vigorously drag your free foot forward on the floor.

ARE YOU FAMILIAR WITH PIPPI LONGSTOCKING, WHO TIED SCRUB-BRUSHES TO HER FEET TO SCRUB THE KITCHEN FLOOR? IMAGINE YOU, TOO, HAVE A BRUSH TIED TO YOUR FOOT AND ARE POLISHING THE FLOOR UNTIL IT SHINES!

DRAG YOUR FOOT WITH SOME FORCE OR THE FLOOR WON'T GET CLEAN!

When your leg is really far forward, only your big toe still touches the floor.

Here, too, your kneecaps are raised.

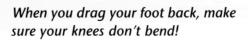

When you drag your foot back, make sure your knees don't bend!

101

TRY IT OUT

Only practicing diligently will bring you success! Sometimes you may think: "I won't be able to do it anyway! It just doesn't work for me!" But when you keep practicing anyway, it will continue to get better.

No one was born a master! Even the best dancers practice a lot every day.

Exercises in a sitting position with the legs extended in front

Before you practice the Battement Tendu, do a few exercises in a sitting position with your legs extended in front of you. You will regain the feel for the extension of the feet and toes. Be sure to keep your posture erect!

Flex your feet.

Point your feet and toes and bend them toward the floor.

Painting and dabbing with pointed feet

Imagine your pointed foot is a paintbrush with which you are dabbing little dots onto the floor. Or "draw" a picture on the floor with your big toe. Who can guess what you "drew?"

STRETCHING EXERCISES

You start by sitting in a wide straddle. The back is straight and the knees are extended.

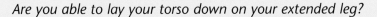

To the side

Now bend over one leg and slowly let your fingers walk down to your feet.

Are you able to lay your torso down on your extended leg?

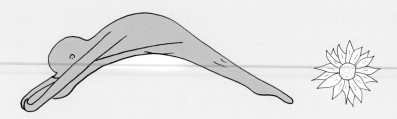

Now try it on the other side.

To the middle

From the straddle position, slowly bend over in the center and let your fingers continue to walk forward. How far can you go?

Keep in mind:
Your muscles must be warmed up before you do the stretching exercises. When muscles and ligaments are not supple, you can get hurt!

JUMPS
(SAUTÉ, PRONOUNCE: SAW-TAY)

Jumps allow the dancers to show that they are not only able to do delicate, gentle movements. The jump is fast and powerful, but is supposed to look light and smooth.

The starting point for the jump is the bending of the knees. To do this, you have already practiced the bending of the legs, **Demi-Plié**.

IN CLASSICAL BALLET, THE AUDIENCE IS PARTICULARLY DELIGHTED WHEN THE JUMPS ARE VERY HIGH AND POWERFUL.

BUT AT THE SAME TIME, EVERYTHING HAS TO LOOK EFFORTLESS — AS IF THE DANCERS ARE FLYING.

In the parallel position

Once again, you start the exercises in the parallel position. You can rest your hands on your hips or practice with your arms at your side.

105

In 1st position

You stand in first position, jump straight up, and land again in first position.

You can also:

- *jump up from first position,*
- *open the legs during the jump and land in second position.*

Bend the knees before the jump.

The heels "push" you off the floor.

In 2nd position

You get in second position, jump straight up and land again in second position.

You can also:

- *jump from second position,*
- *close the legs during the jump, and land in first position.*

107

TRY IT OUT

For jumping, you need strong muscles and a good sense of balance.

Hop over the puddle!

Imagine there is a big puddle and you are jumping over it, from one leg to the other – without getting wet.

Ribbit, ribbit ... Jump like a frog!

You get into a low, wide squat. Now leap like a frog. As you jump, extend your legs – you want to go far!

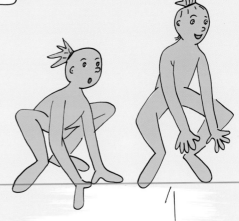

Meow, meow ... Jump like a cat!

Jump from a squat, with your heels still on the floor. Your velvet paws are ready to pounce. Jump like you are jumping over a puddle again and land first on one leg, then on the other leg. The landing is very soft and light, without your feet making a sound on the floor.

Jumping jack

Are you familiar with the jumping jack? When you pull the string, the arms go up and the legs open. If you loosen the string, everything goes back down. So the jumping jack is wide one moment, and narrow the next.

When you are the jumping jack, you jump wide open and then close. Make sure that when you land, your feet always land front to back, and the heels firmly touch down on the floor. If you like, you can clap your hands loudly overhead or against your sides.

Jumping on one leg

Jump only on the right leg.
- How far can you go without stopping?
- How many jumps can you do without a break?
- Now jump only on the left leg. Is it easier or harder?

Maybe you have noticed that jumping on the right leg is easier than on the left leg. That's normal – just like there are right-handed and left-handed people. But try to practice especially on the "weaker" leg.

109

WHAT YOU CAN DO ALREADY

During your dance practices, you will continue to learn and try out more and more movements. Some already work pretty well and some not quite so well!

In the following boxes, you will find all of the principles of dance we have described in the book.

Fill in the flower as much as you think you are able to do the item that is listed. Use the blank lines to give yourself some praise or write down practice tips.

Two boxes are totally blank. You can fill them out when you have learned some more movements.

Look at how Gracie filled out her flower:

FLYING

- *THE TAKEOFF TO FLY IS REALLY FAST.*
- *I CAN FLAP MY WINGS BEAUTIFULLY.*
- *SOMETIMES I AM TOO HASTY.*
- *MY EYES ARE NOT ALWAYS LOOKING STRAIGHT AHEAD. IT'S POSSIBLE THAT I MIGHT HIT A TREE SOME DAY.*
- *I NEED TO WORK ON MY LANDINGS.*

 LEARNING BALLET

ERECT POSTURE

_____

_____

STRAIGHTENING THE LEGS

_____

_____

FLEXING AND POINTING THE FEET

_____

_____

LEG POSITIONS

_____

_____

BENDING THE KNEES (DEMI-PLIÉ)

_____

_____

GETTING ON THE BALL OF THE FOOT (RELEVÉ)

_____

_____

BENDING OVER IN A SITTING POSITION WITH LEGS EXTENDED FORWARD

_____

_____

BENDING OVER FROM A STANDING POSITION

_____

_____

DRAGGING THE FOOT (BATTEMENT TENDU)

_____

_____

JUMPS

_____

_____

_____

_____

_____

_____

WHO IS DANCING ON THIS BEAUTIFUL STAGE?

On these pages, you can create a dance of your own. Draw the dancers with the appropriate costumes. Don't forget the backdrop!

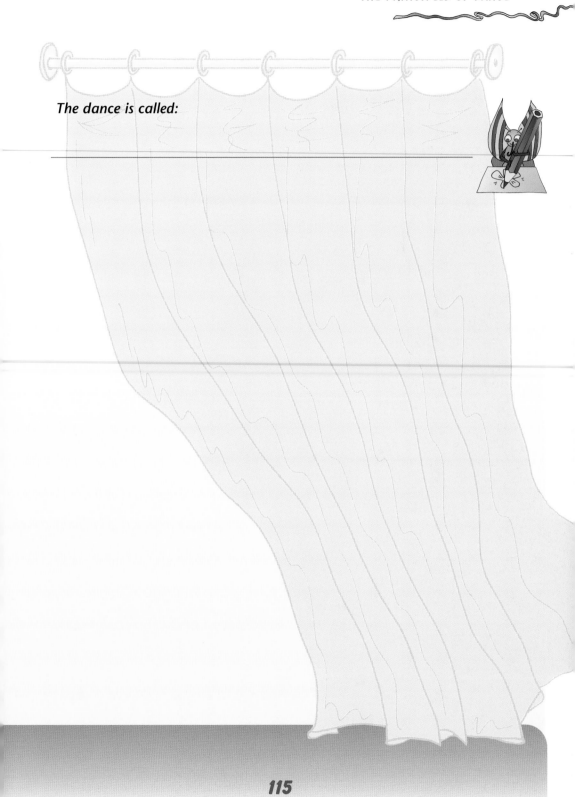

The dance is called:

_____

THE DANCE QUIZZ

We have listed four possible answers to each question. But only one of the four answers is correct. Can you find it?

 1 **What is another word for a dance shoe?**

A Rubber boot   B Slipper

C Flip-flop   D Sandal

2 **What do you call the frilly skirt of a ballerina?**

A Tattoo   B Mini skirt

C Tofu   D Tutu

3 **What is the French word for 1st position**

A En première   B Numero uno

C Baguette   D Heinie

4 **What does "half pointe" mean?**

A Short performance   B Little applause

C Balls of the feet   D Small sword

8 DANCING TOGETHER IS FUN

At some point you will realize that you really enjoy dancing. You want to dance and move to music all the time. But soon your room and the living room carpet aren't enough anymore.

You want to practice together with others and prepare with your group for a great performance. Now it is also important that a dance instructor shows you the proper exercises, pays attention to the correct execution of the movements, and makes suggestions.

Now the time has come to sign up for classes!

HOW DO I FIND THE RIGHT CLASS?

You can learn to dance with different groups. There are classes at athletic organizations, music schools, or ballet schools. Maybe friends or acquaintances have a suggestion.

Most groups will let you get "a little taste" first. That means you can just try it out to see if you like it.

Don't forget, at first everything is new and different. The exercises are unfamiliar and you don't understand some of the directions very well. That's normal and will soon change!

Once you have a "little taste," ask yourself the following questions:

- Do you like the dance studio?
- Is the instructor nice?
- Is the instructor able to explain the exercises well and does he or she help you with them?
- Will I find friends here?
- Do the other children feel comfortable here and have fun practicing?

If you answered "Yes" to these questions, you have found the right place. Now have fun!

Unlike the instruction at school, your parents have to pay for these lessons. But they will do so gladly when they see that you enjoy dancing so much and practice diligently.

BALLET SCHOOLS

ADOLESCENTS WHO HAD DANCE LESSONS AS CHILDREN CAN APPLY AT A BALLET SCHOOL. AN APTITUDE TEST DETERMINES IF THEY POSSESS THE PHYSICAL REQUIREMENTS FOR BALLET TRAINING. IN ADDITION TO THE PRINCIPLES OF DANCE, THE BALLET STUDENTS MUST ALSO DEMONSTRATE MUSICALITY, THE ABILITY TO IMPROVISE DANCE, AND EXPRESSIVENESS.

ANYONE WHO PASSES THE TEST CAN BEGIN TRAINING AS A PROFESSIONAL DANCER AT THE BALLET SCHOOL. EVERY DAY AFTER SCHOOL, BALLET STUDENTS PRACTICE SEVERAL HOURS AT THE DANCE STUDIO. THAT LEAVES THEM VERY LITTLE FREE TIME.

THE TRAINING SPANS SEVERAL YEARS AND REQUIRES MUCH DILIGENCE, STRENGTH, AND STAMINA. GRADUATES OF A BALLET SCHOOL CAN LATER DANCE FOR A BALLET OR DANCE COMPANY, AN OPERA HOUSE, OR A THEATER.

MY FIRST DANCE GROUP

Here I am learning: _____

My first day was on: _____

My dance instructor's name is:

_____

Here you can paste a photo of your group or the logo of your dance school.

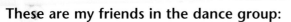

These are my friends in the dance group:
(On this page you can collect signatures from all of your friends in the dance group.)

Gracie

EVERYONE WANTS TO HAVE FUN

First we want to tell you about a strange dance group. Do you see what's going on here?

What is going on here?

The dance instructor has already started with the warm-up, when Tina comes running up to the group in her street shoes to quickly get the key to the locker room. Tom isn't able to jump very well because he is finishing his apple, Mia and Julie are talking loudly, Kim is crying because her jeans are too tight to stretch in, and Anne slipped and fell in the apple juice that Tanya spilled ...

Do you think that learning in this group would be fun? Surely not! Well, to be honest, we made this story up. No place is that bad! Or is there maybe just a little bit of truth there?

Rules are necessary

To make sure all children enjoy practicing and can learn well, there are rules for dance lessons. These rules are set by the instructor and discussed with the group. All of the dancers make sure that the rules are obeyed. This way everyone will have fun practicing.

BALLET STUDIO RULES

We have listed some rules that we think are very important for the group and the dance studio.

☺ Attend practice sessions regularly and punctually. Someone who dawdles misses a lot.

☺ When you are sick, your parents need to notify the dance instructor. If you miss without excuse, no one will know if you will be back to practice soon, or if you will be able to dance in the upcoming performance.

☺ Help each other and be considerate!

☺ Don't talk during instructions and exercises, or you won't understand everything and may make mistakes.

☺ Dress neatly and choose a practical hairstyle! Take off jewelry so it doesn't bother you or get caught on something!

☺ Street shoes are not allowed on the dance floor!

☺ There is no eating or chewing gum in the dance studio.

☺ The ballet bars (barres) are not for gymnastics! What other rules do you have? Write them down on the blank lines!

☺ _____

☺ _____

☺ _____

What other rules do you have? Write them down on the blank lines!

THE BIG PERFORMANCE

A big event for any dance group is performing together. Now you can show your parents, grandparents, siblings, and friends what you have learned during those many practice sessions. Often it is a Christmas story or a spring dance, or maybe even the final dance recital. You have prepared a long time for this.

Butterflies in the stomach

Now the big day has finally come. Your parents dress up and even your little brother looks presentable today. Your bag is packed and you're ready to go. Your dance instructor welcomes you, the costumes are handed out, some dancers get their make-up done, and you warm up.

But what's this? There is a fluttering in your tummy! This strange sensation, that you have suddenly forgotten everything, your legs get very heavy, or you constantly have to run to the restroom. Even the biggest performers have it. This nervousness before the performance is called **stage fright**.

But if you practiced and are prepared, you won't need to worry. As soon as the performance begins it will be over and you will have danced beautifully. And if something does go wrong? No problem! Just keep on going; almost no one in the audience noticed.

RELYING ON EVERYONE

To have a successful and nice performance, it is important that you attend the dance lessons regularly. Particularly during the rehearsal stage, everyone has an important place. If you are not ready, the others will not be able to practice very well.

Whether you dance a leading part or a bit part, every dancer is important! Only when everyone does his or her best, will the performance be successful. That includes:

- Attending practice sessions regularly.
- Being on time and well prepared for the performance.
- Not getting upset about the mistakes others make, but rather helping them! You might make mistakes, too!

The big, long applause from the audience at the end of the dance will be your reward! You can proudly take a bow in front of everyone.

125

Find the differences!

At first glance, these two drawings look identical.

But there are 11 differences. Can you find them?

9 FIT AND HEALTHY

Movement is good for the body. You move when you run, jump, swim, bike, play ball, and of course when you dance. It is how you toughen up your body, strengthen your muscles, your lungs, your circulation, and your immune system.

You will stay fit and healthy. Couch potatoes become lazy and dull.

IF YOU MOVE, YOU HAVE TO EAT

Dancing is fun, but it is also pretty strenuous! That is why your body needs energy. You get that through nutrition.

Slim and healthy

Surely you have noticed that most dancers are pretty slim. Their slender bodies make the movements look much more graceful and lovely. A plump dancer appears more like a bear lumbering through the forest. Doing the jumps, spins, and bends is more difficult for her and she gets winded more easily.

But that won't happen to you if you eat healthy. Eat things like fresh fruit, vegetables, whole grain bread, or yogurt. They will give you the energy your body needs. Greasy fries or sausage, cake, cookies, or chocolate should only be eaten in small amounts. They contain too much fat and sugar. If you pay attention to that, it won't be too difficult to stay at a healthy weight.

Don't forget: You are still doing lots of growing, learning, playing, and especially dancing. For that your body needs that important energy.

If you don't eat, you'll feel listless and will get sick!

IF YOU SWEAT, YOU HAVE TO DRINK REGULARLY

When you sweat while you dance, your leotard is often soaked and you can see beads of perspiration on your skin.

Sweating isn't bad – it's even healthy. But your body now lacks the fluids you lose when you sweat. So now you have to drink a lot so your body will once again have enough fluids.

The best thirst quenchers

Pure juice and soft drinks are not suitable for replenishing fluids. They contain too much sugar.

Instead, drink:

- Water
- Mineral water
- Water and juice mix (apple, orange or cherry juice diluted with water)
- Herbal or fruit tea (also sweetened with honey)

When you are thirsty and drink, you have to be careful not to drink too hastily. It is better to take smaller sips more often. Be careful not to fill your stomach so full that you will barely be able to move!

HELLO, DOCTOR!

Exercise is fun and healthy! There is nothing better you can do for your body!

But if you are not sure whether the movements in dance are good for you, ask your pediatrician. He will do a physical examination, look at your spine, and give you nutritional tips.

Any good dance instructor also knows about the physical development of children, and will look out for you. He also knows that the growth of bones and joints must reach a certain point before you can begin dancing en pointe.

DON'T FORGET TO WARM UP

Your dance instructor will likely include a warm-up at the beginning of your lesson.

It is important that your muscles are made warm, limber, and supple through various exercises. It will help protect you from injury.

To warm up your muscles, you can run and skip, bend and stretch, and afterwards shake out your limbs really well!

Remember to warm up when you practice at home!

A SUCCESSFUL DAY BEGINS WITH A GOOD START IN THE MORNING!

A few tips from Gracie:

- Go to bed on time and get plenty of sleep!

- Look forward to the new day.

- Stretch after getting up. How about some morning calisthenics?

- A cold shower is ideal after washing. It is refreshing and toughens you up.

- Whole grain bread, granola, cornflakes, milk, yogurt and fresh fruit are all part of a good and healthy breakfast.

- Don't forget to brush your teeth after you eat!

This dancer is very hungry after practicing. She would love to eat everything all at once. What would you recommend? Cross out anything you think isn't very healthy!

Which food should you eat more of during the day and as a snack when you are hungry in between meals? Cross out every L, Y, M, A, X, E, K, and D, and read the remaining letters.

F	D	K	A	R	E	X	Y	M	L	A
M	E	L	M	A	U	D	I	K	D	Y
Y	A	D	D	L	K	Y	M	A	M	T

10 LITTLE DICTIONARY

All people all over the world understand the "language of dance." It doesn't matter what their native language is.

> **SALUT, MON AMI!**

> **HELLO, FRIENDS!**

It is important that dancers from different countries can communicate about the movements. Successful dancers often work in other countries.

In classical ballet, the principal language is French, and important movements have French names. Modern dance often uses English terminology.

Perhaps you have already heard some of these terms from your dance instructor.

133

Barre. . . . . This is the bar at the dance studio that you can hold on to.

Battement Tendu. . . . . Dragging the foot

Choreographer . . . . He plans the dance and determines the steps of the dancers

Demi-Plié . . . . Bending the knees

En face. . . . . Facing forward

En première . . . . First position

En seconde. . . . . Second position

En troisième. . . . . Third position

Exercise . . . . Practicing a movement

Flex. . . . . Angling the foot

Grand-Jeté . . . . Big jump

Pas de Deux. . . . . Two people dancing together.

Petit-Jeté . . . . Small jump on one leg

Plié . . . . Knee bend

Pirouette . . . . Turn

Première. . . . . First performance of a dance

Prima ballerina . . . . Ballerina dancing the principal part in a ballet

Relevé . . . . Getting up on the balls of the feet

Roll-up . . . . Bending over with a rounded back

Sauté . . . . Jump

Use the blank lines to write down other terms you want to memorize. Be aware that the pronunciation of these words is different than their spelling.

SONGS AND POEMS

People can express their emotions very well through music and dance. That is probably why there are so many songs about them.

The Chicken Dance

Ring Around the Rosie

If You're Happy and You Know it

Twinkle-Twinkle Little Star

I'm a Little Tea Pot

The Wheels on the Bus

Do you know any other dance songs? Write them down here!

My best friends

When I'm cheerful or sad,
When I'm angry or happy,
Music is my buddy
And dance is my friend

I want to spin, float, stomp,
Jump, skip, and be merry.
I want to show my feelings
And my friends will be there with me.

Dancing is a wonderful way to express your feelings.

Try writing a poem about it, if you like. Paste it in here!

11 SOLUTIONS

On the following pages, you will find the solutions to the brainteasers.

Here we also explain what the little mistake manikins are doing wrong. We often intentionally exaggerated some things about the mistake manikins. But this way you can recognize the mistakes more easily.

Pg. 22   Clown, House, Ostrich, Rabbit, Egg, Ostrich, Guitar, Rabbit, Apple, Purse, Hat, Egg, Rabbit

The solution is:

C H O R E O G R A P H E R

FIRE BIRD

NUT CRACKER

SWAN LAKE

SLEEPING BEAUTY

Pg. 24

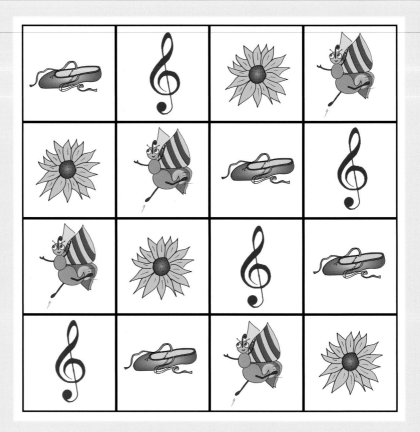

Pg. 34

Pg. 50

Pg. 60/61   **Mistakes with erect posture**

1   Rounded back with droopy shoulders.
2   The eyes are on the floor and not looking straight ahead.
3   The knees are not straight.
4   This manikin has a hollow back instead of a straight back.
5   Knees and feet are not closed.
6   Well, this doesn't have anything to do with erect posture.

Pg. 74   **Mistakes with the parallel position**

1   The legs are not straight and the knees are not closed.
2   The body weight is not on the whole foot, but on the outside edges.
3   The feet are not closed.

Pg. 75   **Mistakes with 1st position**

1   Legs and feet are not closed.
2   The back is not straight.

Pg. 75   **Mistakes with 2nd position**

3   The feet are not turned out, but point to the inside.
4   Too much distance between the feet. It should be approximately one foot length.
5   The knees are not straight.

Pg. 82/83   **Mistakes with bending the knees**

1   Rounded back.
2   The feet are not standing on the entire sole, but only on the outside edges.
3   The dancer doesn't have the heels on the floor.
4   Even for second position, the distance between the heels is too great.
5   The knees are not bent evenly.
6   The dancer is not looking straight ahead, but down.

Pg. 94   **Mistakes with bending over in sitting position with legs extended forward**

1   The knees are not straight.
2   The heels are not on the floor.
3   The head is turned up.

Pg. 95   **Mistakes with bending over from a standing position**

1   The knees are not straight.
2   The heels are not on the floor.
3   The head is turned up.

Pg. 116
1 **B** – Slippers
2 **D** – Tutu
3 **A** – En Première
4 **C** – Balls of the feet

Pg. 126

Pg. 132

F	D	K	A	R	E	X	Y	M	L	A
M	E	L	M	A	U	D	I	K	D	Y
Y	A	D	D	L	K	Y	M	A	M	T

The solution is F R U I T

12 LET'S TALK

If this were a book for adults, these pages for the parents and dance instructors would of course appear at the very front of the book as the preface. But since it is a book for children, we are putting this chapter at the end, sort of as an addendum.

Our beginning dancers are all preschool or elementary school students, who are just learning to read and have not yet had very much exposure to books. They are absolutely in need of support from big people who can help them with the approach to the book.

The best way to start is by leafing through the book and looking at the pictures, and filling in and recording information. This book does not have to be read back to back, but is also very useful as a reference work and diary.

Have fun reading together!

DEAR PARENTS

Do you remember the first time your little daughter or son moved to music, twirled around and made clumsy little hops? Most likely you will say: As soon as my child could walk! Your child kept its fascination with moving to music and now it wants to take dance lessons.

She wants to learn dance movements from an experienced dance instructor together with other children and prepare with the group for fine performances. It is nice that you want to support your child as she learns those first dance steps.

Dance is a wonderful opportunity for expressing emotions and moods, joy, anger, fun, lightness, rage, sorrow, exuberance – everything can be "danced out." The shy child has an opportunity to become more outgoing and the more exuberant child will find an outlet. Dance can become an individual form of expression and creativity while still encouraging a sense of community.

Dancing and the exercises at the lessons promote body awareness, endurance, dexterity, strength and flexibility. Children improve their sense of rhythm and their ability to concentrate.

Your child is part of a social community and learns about the peculiarities of the group, as well as the significance of the soloist. She learns discipline, empathy and self-confidence. She will have success and also recognize that others are sometimes better. At times she will have the leading role and other times a bit part. Handling these emotions isn't easy. But your child will learn to do so and thus firmly establish her identity.

Personal responsibility must be learned. By and by, the little dancers look after the care and completeness of their clothing and pay attention to punctuality and regularity with respect to practice sessions and performances. So encourage your child as she learns those first dance steps, practices and rehearses.

In the beginning, the little dancers' delight in moving, skipping and twirling will outweigh anything else. Of course this also requires some basic dance principles. The dance instructor will ensure a balance between the practice of the basic dance principles and actual dancing.

The children should have fun and develop their skills at the same time. That is also the purpose of our book. In addition to the explanations of essential principles, the children obtain lots of information about dancing in general. They have the opportunity to get actively involved with their hobby.

Be helpful, but with prudence!

Do not let your expectations for your child get too high! What matters most is the joy of moving and dancing. Excessive ambition would only be harmful. Don't compare your child to others of the same age, because biological development, particularly at this age, can vary greatly. Just focus on your own child and praise his or her progress. Your child will thank you.

Parental support

Parental support is sought after in dance, as well, be it for organizing the practice outfits, driving to the dance school or the performance location. Parents are in demand for helping to fix hair, apply makeup, and put costumes on. Moms will often help by making costumes, and dads by creating backdrops.

When your child and the others prepare for a performance, it is an integral part of the group. There are no "unimportant parts." Each one has its place and when you are not there, the others cannot practice properly. Therefore the preparation time and the performances are important events in the family's schedule.

But what is better than watching one's eager little dancer dance her part with total concentration? Or how much trust and intimacy there is between parents and children when a little goof-up requires some comforting. Be happy that your child has such a wonderful hobby. Regardless of whether your child will become an internationally celebrated prima ballerina some day or she "only" enjoys the dancing and socializing.

What a children's dance instructor should have:

DEAR DANCE INSTRUCTOR

Surely you'll agree that it feels great to look at these tots with their excited faces and expectant eyes. Now it is up to you to introduce them to dancing!

But all children are different. There are self-confident ones and timid ones, the diligent and the not-so-diligent, the talented and the less talented. Each child has her own little personality with individual qualifications and her own developmental history, with hopes and desires, with feelings and needs. We regard them all equally. Children want to be active, to move and have fun. Particularly in a group, they are able to match themselves with their peers and spur each other on.

For beginning dancers, the most important role model is the dance instructor. Children closely observe everything: How he speaks to them, how he gets prepared, and how he performs the movements.

The young dancer is the most important part of the learning and teaching process. The child, no matter how young and how much of a beginner she may be, is always subject to her own development and never just the object of our influence. Therefore, offer them enough advice and opportunities for their own development. Foster and utilize your little beginning dancers' independence. Take the path from directing to inspiring. The children don't have to and aren't supposed to, but they can and they may.

The value of this little book

The value of this little book will depend entirely on how you will integrate it into the instruction. It is written specifically for children who are beginning dancers. But it can also be recommended to parents who wish to accompany their child on this path.

The book focuses on the children's needs and is intended to help them engage in dancing outside of the studio, as well. The child acquires a fairly complete foundation for practicing via the book's illustrations and descriptions. She will be better able to follow your explanations and demonstrations. The young dancers can review at their leisure what they have learned, keep track of goals and learning progress, and receive suggestions for practicing at home and with other children. This develops the ability to act independently and accelerates the learning process

An environment is created in which the children themselves, step by step, think about practicing and learning, their movements and actions, and finally monitor and evaluate their behavior. They become a partner to the dance instructor. We would like the children to enjoy coming to practice and go home with a sense of achievement. And of course that would make the practice sessions fun for the dance instructor as well.

The book and the dance lesson

Tell the children that this book will be their personal companion while they learn to dance. Give them the logo of their dance facility and a photo to paste in the book. This will boost their attachment to you and the group.

Help the children to use this book properly. In the beginning, read some segments together and explain to the children how the photos and illustrations should be viewed and understood. Together with the children, make entries regarding goals, suggestions, tips on how to correct mistakes, etc. In doing so, you create critical orientation aids for their understanding and independent practicing.

With the aid of this book, you can also assign homework for the next practice session. The children read up on a topic and get to do a show-and-tell at the next session.

Dear Dance and Ballet Instructor, it already became apparent during the preparation phase of this book, that it would not be easy! Our intentions were clear, but not only are there many different children's dance schools and facilities, but there are just as many different views on dance or ballet for children.

But we don't want to write a "textbook" or a methodological tutorial for teachers, but rather give children a companion. It is a reference work, a diary, a specialized book with lots of content about the principles of dance and dancing in general. We want to motivate the little dancers to actively participate in the learning process. If you would like to add something or would prefer to use different terminology, let your children write it in the book.

We wish you lots of fun and joy,
and of course successful performances
with your little charges.

PHOTO & ILLUSTRATION CREDITS

Cover design:	Jens Vogelsang, Aachen
Illustrations:	Katrin Barth
Cover photo:	Front – dpa Picture Alliance, Frankfurt, Germany
	Back – Stefan Göök
Photos (inside):	Berndt Barth, Stefan Göök, Ralph Grabow, Karl-Heinz Sandner, Rainer Schilling, Markus R. Wiese